DATE DUE

DEC 19			

DEMCO 38-297

ED EMBERLEY'S

A B C

LITTLE, BROWN AND COMPANY
BOSTON — TORONTO

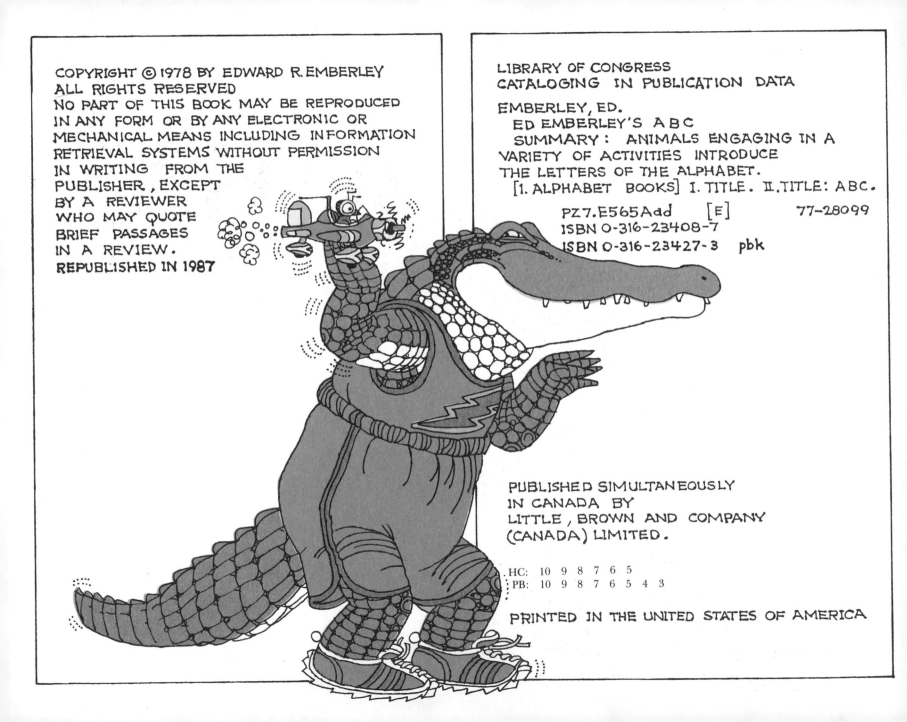

LIBRARY OF CONGRESS
CATALOGING IN PUBLICATION DATA

EMBERLEY, ED.
  ED EMBERLEY'S A B C
  SUMMARY: ANIMALS ENGAGING IN A
VARIETY OF ACTIVITIES INTRODUCE
THE LETTERS OF THE ALPHABET.
  [1. ALPHABET BOOKS] I. TITLE. II. TITLE: ABC.

PZ7.E565Aad   [E]   77-28099
ISBN 0-316-23408-7
ISBN 0-316-23427-3   pbk

PUBLISHED SIMULTANEOUSLY
IN CANADA BY
LITTLE, BROWN AND COMPANY
(CANADA) LIMITED.

HC: 10 9 8 7 6 5
PB: 10 9 8 7 6 5 4 3

PRINTED IN THE UNITED STATES OF AMERICA

ANT

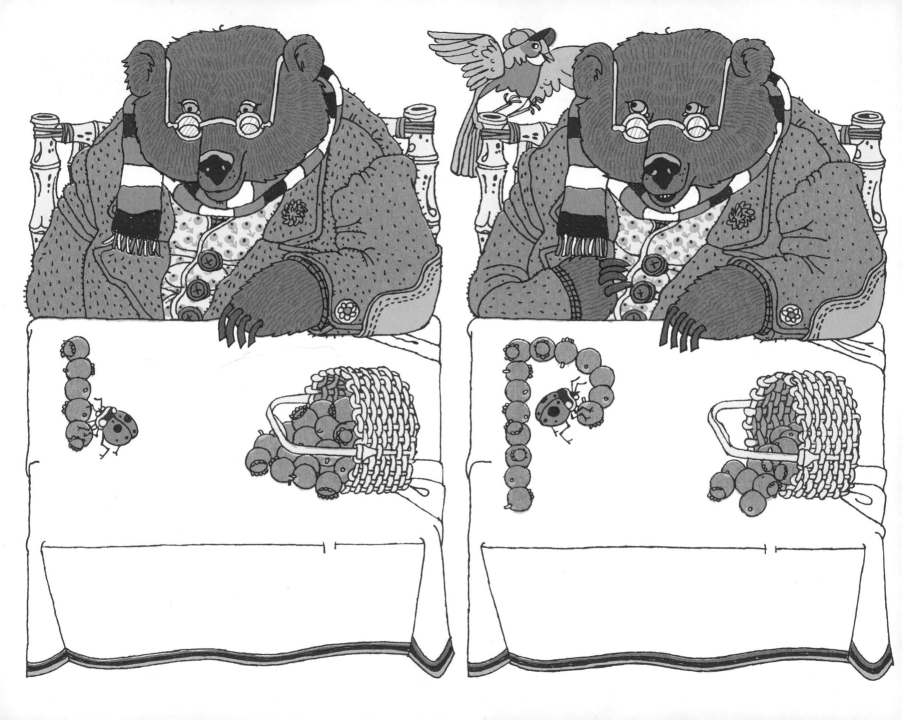

BEAR

CROW

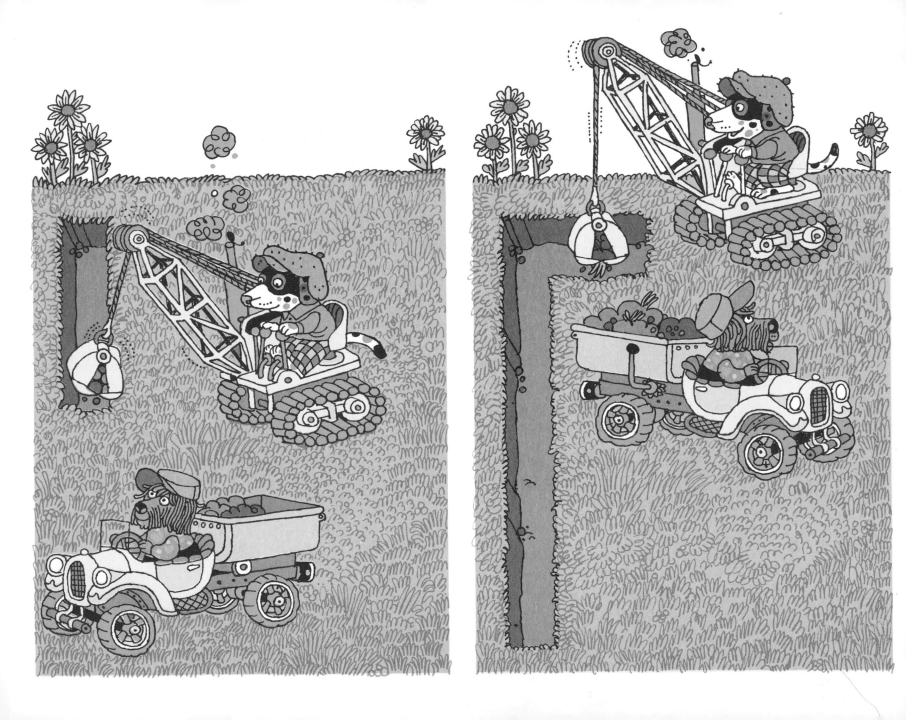

DOGS

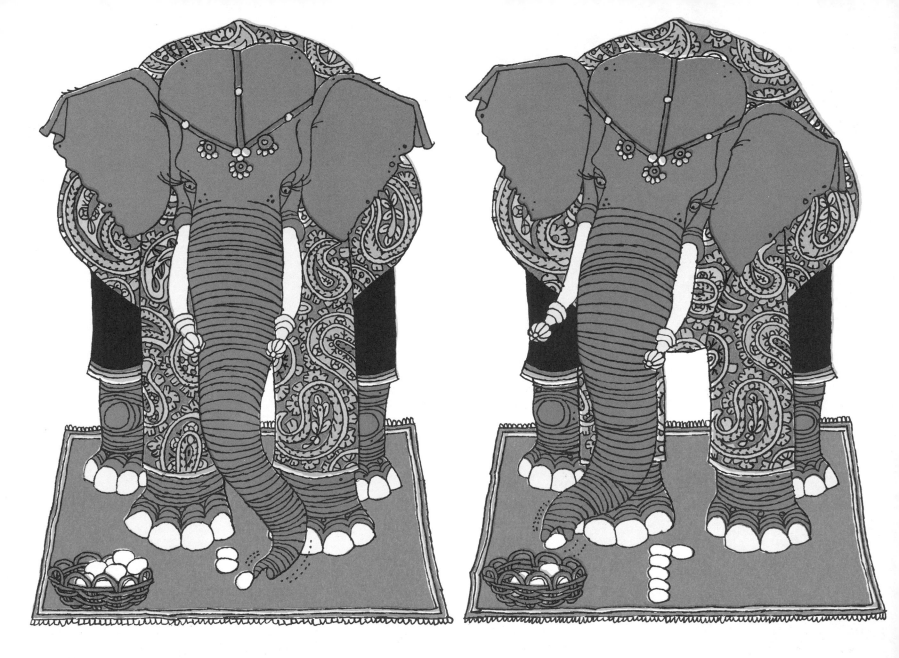

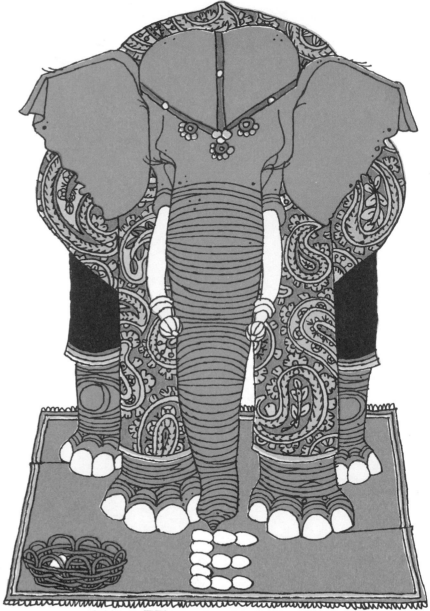

ELEPHANT

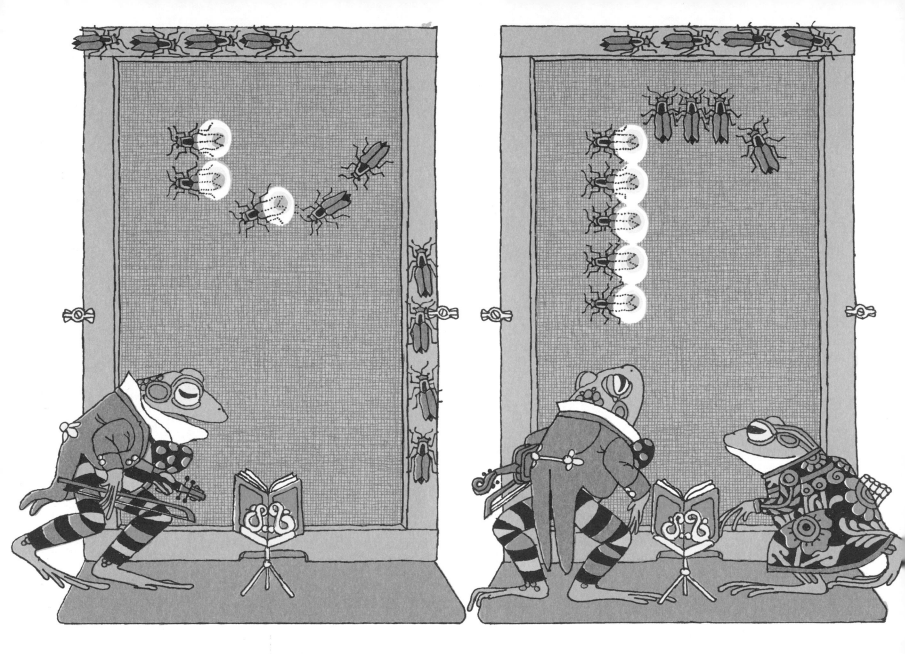

FROGS

GEESE

HEN

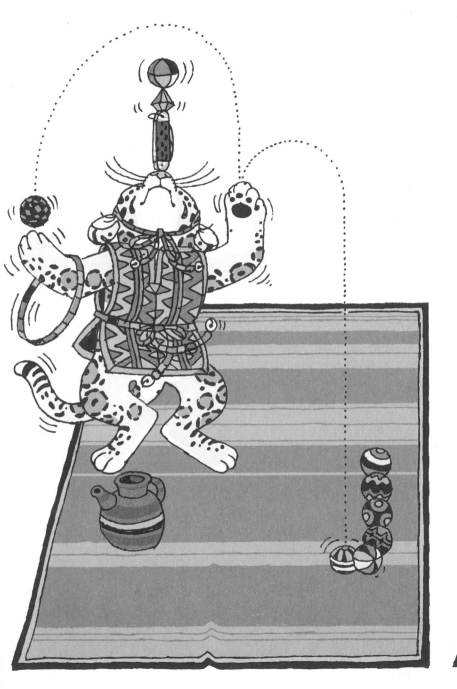
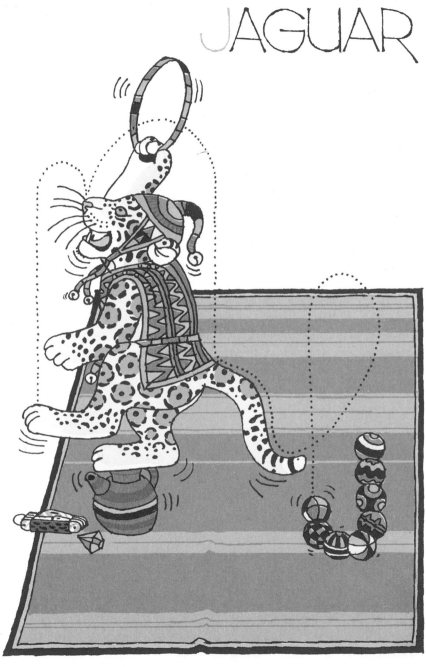

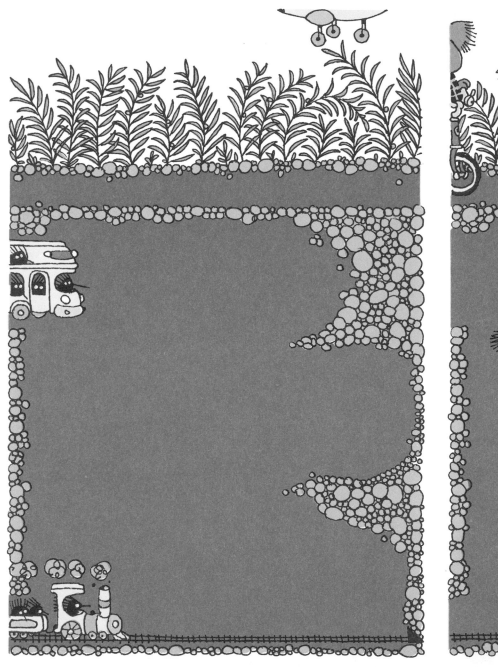

KIWI

MICE

LION

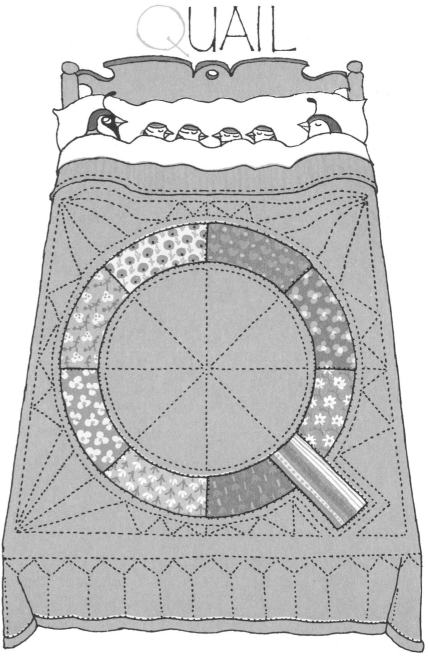

RABBIT

SNAILS

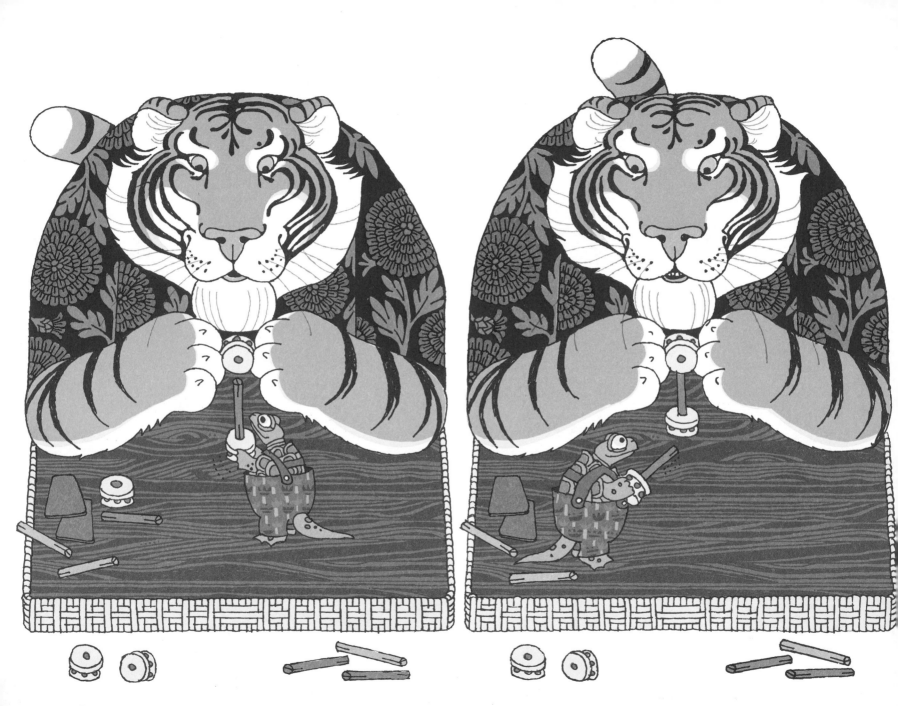

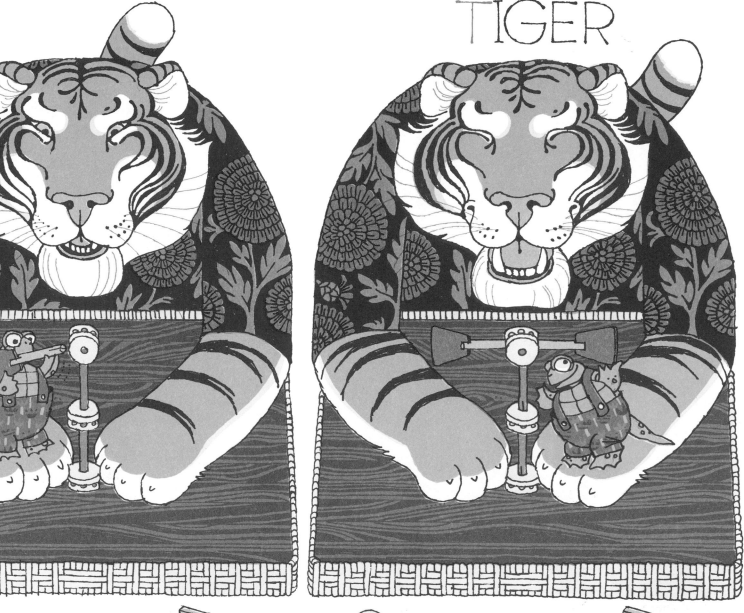

VOLE

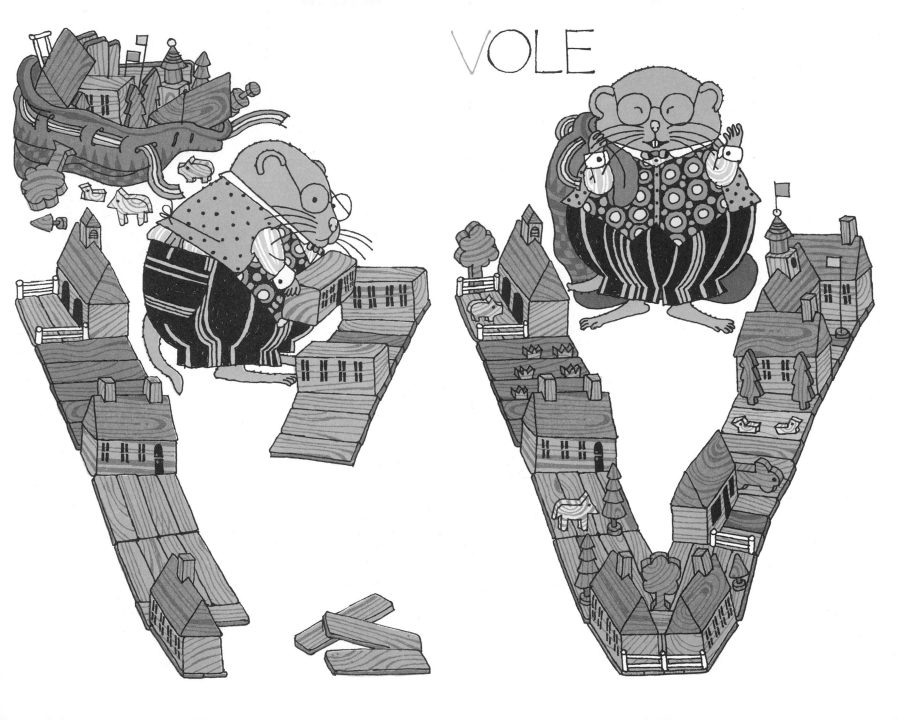

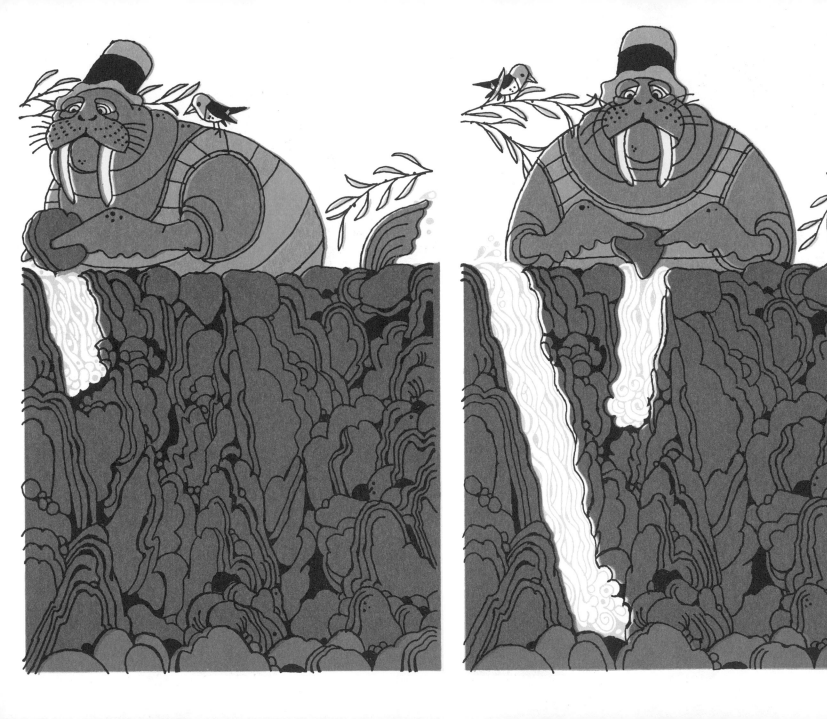

WALRUS

YAK

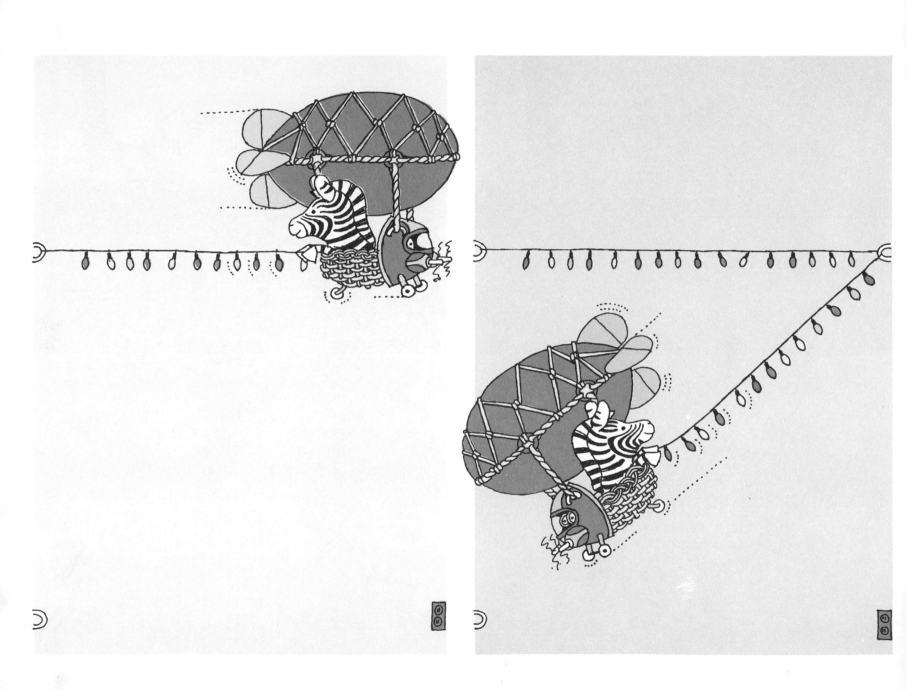

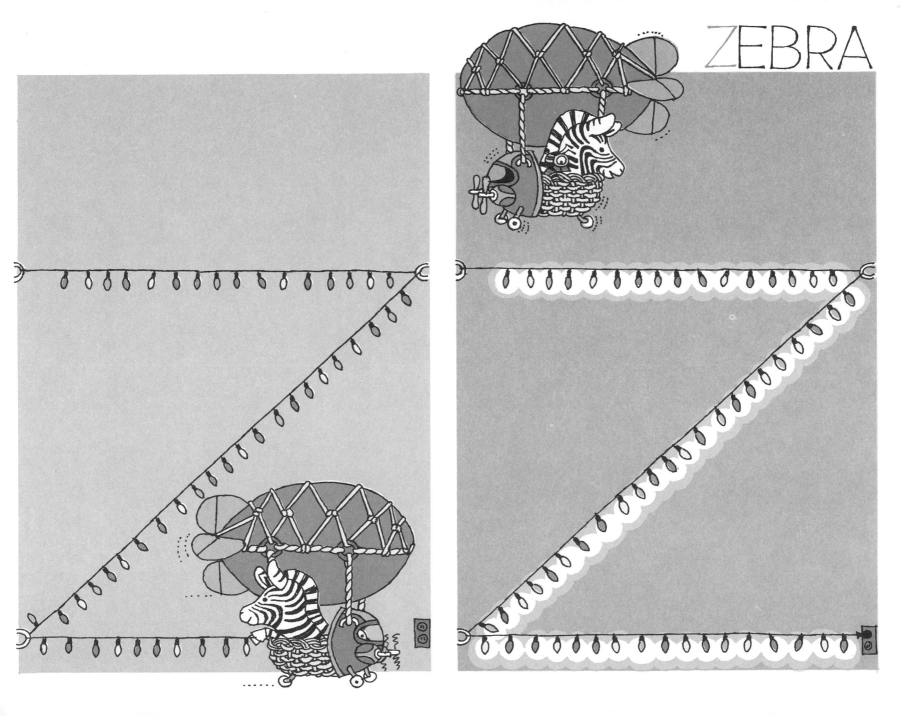

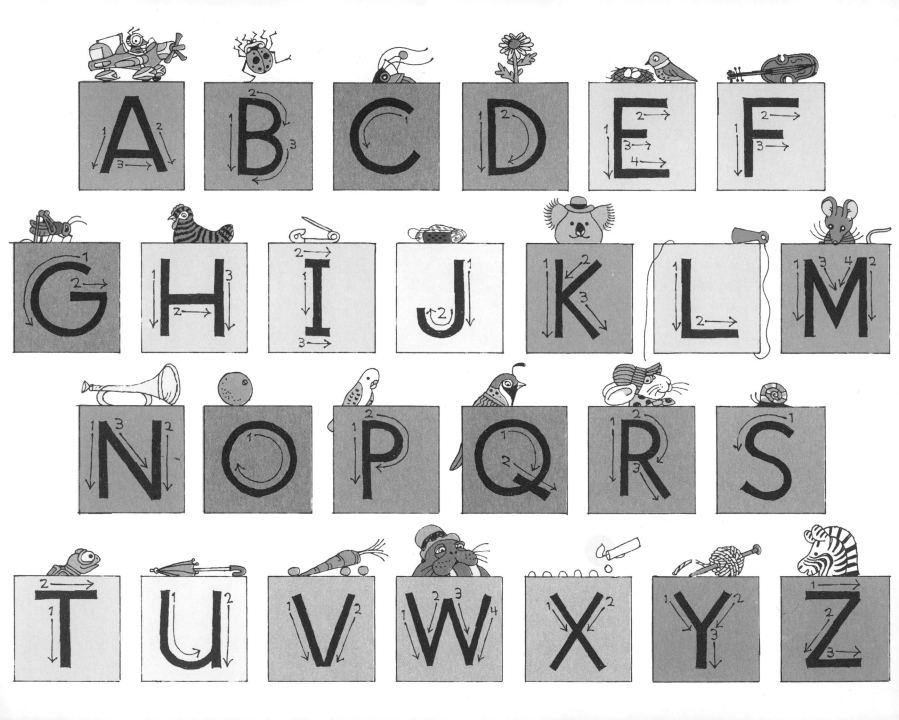

SOME THINGS FOR YOU TO FIND.

A ANT, ALLIGATOR, AIRPLANE.
B BEAR, BAMBOO, BASKET, BUG, BIRD,
  BLUE, BROWN, BLACK, BERRIES.
C CROW CRICKET, CORN, CLOWN.
D DOG, DIGGING, DINOSAUR (BONES)
  DAISY, DUMP TRUCK.
E ELEPHANT, EGGS, ELEVEN.
F FROG, FIREFLIES, FLOWERS, FIDDLE,
  FIVE, FOUR.
G GOOSE, GANDER, GOSLING, GEESE,
  GOLF, GRASS, GRASSHOPPER,
  GREEN, GRAY, GRAPES, GERANIUMS.
H HORSE, HEN, HAY, HOOF, HELPING.
★ I PIG, PIN, PINK, RIBBON.
J JAGUAR, JUG, JUGGLER,
  JEWEL, JACKKNIFE.
K KIWI, KOALA, KANGAROO.
L LIZARD, LOBSTER, LINE, LITTLE.
M MICE, MOUSE, MOTHER, MAIL.
★ N LION, RACOON, RIBBON, LEMON, GREEN,
  BROWN, FAN, MOON, CAN, SPOON,
O OWL, ORANGE, ORANGUTAN.
P PARROT, PIRATE, PINK, PURPLE, PAINT,
  PUFFIN, PAIR, PARAKEETS.
Q QUAIL, QUILT.
R RABBIT, ROBOT, RED, ROLLER.

S SNAIL, SINGING, SILENT, SIX,
  SEVEN, SUBMARINE, SALAMANDER,
  SAILOR, STRING, STONES.
T TIGER, TURTLE, TRAY.
★ U UNICORN, UNICYCLE, UMBRELLA,
  2 UKELELE (ONE YELLOW, ONE BLACK)
  UNGUICULATE.
V VOLE, VILLAGE, VEST, VEGETABLES,
W WALRUS, WATERFALL,
  WILLOW, WOODPECKER.
★ X FOX, BOX, AX, WAX, SIX.
Y YAK, YELLOW, YARN.
Z ZEBRA, ZEPPELIN.

BARBARA AND ED EMBERLEY, THEIR MARK

ART WORK FINISHED, CAMERA READY
JANUARY 18, 1978
BLACK LINE DRAWINGS BY ED EMBERLEY,
COLOR OVERLAYS BY BARBARA EMBERLEY,
COLOR OVERLAYS FOR BEAR AND RABBIT
PAGES BY MICHAEL EMBERLEY.